Anayo · Kalisha · Cleo · Elijah & Abigail
Tiarni & Kiarni · Nevaeh · Kayin · Kaylia · Ava-Marie
Renell · Shaddai · Makai · Aniyah · Theodore
Ziah · Lewis · Niara · Diego · Mylee
Jamil · Jacob · Amirah · Melina · Tinashe

27 Young Writers | 6 to 13 years | 10 boys | 17 girls

From Brent | Dudley | Ealing | Enfield | Essex | Hackney
Haringey | Harrow | Hertfordshire | Islington | Luton
Manchester | Newham | Nottingham | Redbridge | Southwark
Tower Hamlets | Waltham Forest | Gutu, Zimbabwe

First edition printed in 2020 in the United Kingdom
Copyright © 2020 BlackJac Media Limited. All rights reserved
Edited by: Yazmin McKenzie
Illustrations and Design: Ashley Greaves
Sub Editor: Clare Kay
Publisher: BlackJac Media Limited
Designed by: Ashley Greaves

A CIP catalogue record of this book is available from the British Library

ISBN: 9781838094539 PBK
ISBN: 9781838094546 HBK

For orders or enquires, contact:
BlackJac Media: 07429481305

A Covid-19 Project

OUR ROOTS

The inspiring stories of our grandparents and great-grandparents.
A historic collection of profiles written by 27 black children aged between 6 and 13 years.

Edited by Yazmin McKenzie

In memory of Great-grandmother Reverend Benita Elenora Foster
Sunrise 28 September 1930 to Sunset 17 July 2020
Nana passed away after being interviewed by her great-granddaughter Mylee Campbell

A Covid-19 Project

We called this a Covid-19 Project because of the time. Coronavirus has been for many a challenging experience: isolation, not being able to hug loved ones, fear and indeed even the death of loved ones. It was a time that was associated with so many negative connotations, so when the announcement came on 18 March that all schools in the UK would close from the afternoon of 20 March, except for vulnerable children and the children of key workers, it presented the perfect opportunity to involve children in something positive.

Exams had been cancelled, so many schoolchildren were expected to download worksheets from school websites and work independently. Parents were struggling to teach their children, while working from home, so welcomed the opportunity for their children to take part in a project that would leave a legacy.

A list of 99 questions was created by the youngsters themselves and, after some training, they selected at least 40 questions to ask their grandparents, and then contacted their grandparents via Facebook, WhatsApp Video, Skype, House Party or Zoom. Our young writers took part in a literacy session, which helped them to structure the profiles of their grandparents, as well as supported them with their spelling, punctuation and grammar. Some of the parents worked with their youngsters to finish off the work.

The final profiles are amazing and we are so proud of our 27 young writers whose work features in our book.

Thankfully, our writers now see a different side to this pandemic. It is a time when they connected with their elders and discovered new things about their grandparents that they probably wouldn't have, if they had not been in lockdown.

Without this precious time, we would not have created this anthology of love.

BlackJac Media: May 2020

DEDICATED TO

Nkechi Ode & Vincent Sabaroche, both stolen from us by Covid-19.

Great-grandma Bailey, great-grandad Bailey, and my beautiful grandmothers
Nanny Lilly & Mama Gem.

Reverend Benita Elenora Foster, who "fought the good fight, finished
the course and kept the faith" and is resting with the Lord after being
interviewed for this book by her great-granddaughter, Mylee.

Our brave Windrush family, who were invited to the UK
and have made a great contribution and massive impact.

And to those, who came to build this country and have been
wrongfully detained, denied legal rights, threatened with deportation,
and wrongfully deported from the UK by the Home Office: Anthony Bryan,
Dexter Bristol, Paulette Wilson and the many more whom this has affected.

We love you!

We salute you!

We thank you.

As a child, I loved listening to my mum and grandmother talk about life in the Caribbean. Mum was born in the UK but always repeated the rich and funny stories that her grandparents told her.

She would tell us about my Nanny Lilly (her mum), who came to the UK from Jamaica in 1965, about how she cried for months, wishing she were back home, living on her sunshine island.

Mum would also break out with the proverbs that her mum had often repeated: "Those, who can't hear, must feel" was a classic, along with "New broom sweep clean but old broom know de corner."

Mum is a retired school senior deputy head and has always talked about wanting to do a project that crossed generations, where the youngsters would learn from the elders and visa versa, and so bridge the generational gap.

Enter: 'Our Roots'! As a family, we all jumped on this journey, with mum doing the training, Romeo organising the paperwork; and I did the editing.

It was a long process through the Coronavirus pandemic and most certainly a labour of love.

When I now read the beautiful stories I can't help but think about my Windrush family, who were treated in a hostile manner by the British government, and who are still fighting for justice and compensation because they have lost their jobs or homes and have been denied benefits and medical treatment to which they were entitled.

BlackJac Media will be donating profits from this book to www.restore-communities.org, a Christian project set up primarily to address some of the needs in black and disadvantaged communities. Their work includes supporting our Windrush families and providing emergency food through community food banks to people who are having difficulty affording food.

Yazmin McKenzie
Editor

CONTENTS

Nan Olga Hettie Garrett *by A'niyah Fenton*..Page 10

Grandad Osa Chris Ikhinmwin *by Abigail and Elijah Ikhinmwin*..............Page 12

Nana Maxine Julie Samuel *by Amirah Edinborough*...............................Page 14

Nanaa Mavis Jones *by Anayo Rose-Morrison*...Page 16

Nana Persis Jackson *by Ava Marie Udeh*..Page 18

Grandad Gladstone Dennis *by Cleo Dennis*..Page 20

Grandad Geeroy Jackson *by Courtney Jackson*......................................Page 22

Granny Cheryl Hernandez *by Diego Ross*...Page 24

Grandad Nick Amaechi Udeh *by Jacob Udeh*...Page 26

Grandad Franklyn Ocarriell McNeilly *by Jamil McNeilly*.......................Page 28

Grandad Vincent Augustus Lewis *by Kalisha Shor Maxam*......................Page 30

Grandad James Uriah Rose *by Kayin Rose-Morrison*..............................Page 32

Grandad Fitzroy Carlton Findlater *by Kaylia Dusauzay*........................Page 34

Grandad Desmond Lloyd *by Lewis Lloyd*..Page 36

Grandma Mary Williams *by Makai Williams*...Page 38

Nana Angela Peart *by Melina Ramirez*..Page 40

Great-Grandmother Reverend Benita Elenora Foster *by Mylee Campbell*....Page 42

Grandad Reverend Sean Samuel *by Nevaeh Bramwell-Thompson*..............Page 44

Great-Grandma Hilda Joyce Baxter *by Niara Pilgrim-Hamilton*...............Page 46

Great-Grandma Ethline Maud Hunter *by Renell Sergeant*.......................Page 48

Nanny Jennifer Hudson *by Shaddai Francis*..Page 50

Grandma Maureen Reid *by Theodore Ashley*...Page 52

Grandma Dolores Edwards *by Tiarni and Kiarni Dawkins*......................Page 54

Grandma Vaida Vongai Makamure *by Tinashe Nduna*............................Page 56

Nana Beverley Michele Steele *by Ziah Anderson-Steele*.........................Page 58

Nan Olga Hettie Garrett

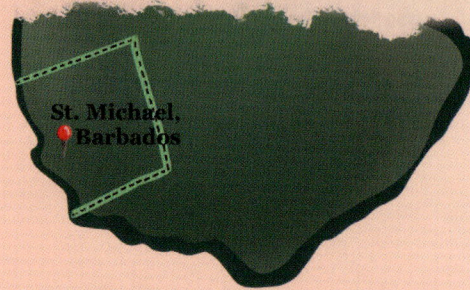

St. Michael, Barbados

My nan's name is Olga Hettie Garrett. Her first name is Russian and her middle name is Hettie, after her grandmother. She is also known as Millar because everyone thought she looked like her mum and her mum's maiden name was Millar. Nan was born on 12 September 1948 in St Michael, Barbados. Her mother's name was Adalin Greenidge and she was a housewife and raised chickens and goats. Adalin lived until the age of 98. Her father's name was Joseph Greenidge and he was a carpenter and raised pigs.

Nan had three brothers and two sisters and she was the fifth child in the family. She grew up in Richmond's Gap, which was a friendly neighbourhood. Nan loved playing outside too! She would collect seashells on the beach and play marbles and jacks; even at night-time. Where she lived was a really safe area and everyone's front door was always left open.

Her brother, Barnford, was a seaman – he would work on the ships for seven months at a time and Nan would be so excited when he was due to come home because he would bring her lots of lovely presents from his travels.

My nan attended Westbury Primary School and St Leonard's Secondary School for Girls and her best friends were Maria and Dianna. The teachers were very strict and if the children were naughty, they would get punished with a beating. As a child, Nan did not have pocket money because her parents didn't have much money.

> "Where she lived was a really safe area and everyone's front door was always left open".

She helped around the house as much as she could though. Her chores were very different to mine! She would fetch and carry water to the house and help clean the pigpen and feed the chickens at the weekend. Nan enjoyed church too and loved taking part in feeding the homeless.

Nan moved to England when she was 18 years old. She had a black and white television, a Hillman Hunter car and her first job was as a nurse at 21 years old. She was paid £28 a month for her nursing job which doesn't sound like much, but back then that was average pay for a skilled worker. She stayed in nursing until she retired.

When she met my grandad Lloyd it was love at first sight. They married in England and had four children: three girls and one boy —my mum Stephanie is the youngest.

My nan loves cricket. Her family name was Greenidge so she tells everyone that the famous Bajan cricketer Sir Cuthbert Gordon Greenidge is her cousin! Nobody knows if he really is our relative, but Nan is convinced it's true. Her favourite food is flying fish and coucou because that is what her mum loved to cook. Her favourite drink is golden apple juice or coconut water because it is refreshing and her favourite film is 'Karate Kid' because it makes her laugh. Grandma's favourite hymn is 'It Is Well With My Soul' because it is a song that makes you feel peaceful and calm when you are feeling down.

Nan has had a few friends, who have died from coronavirus, so she found the Covid-19 lockdown very scary. She is sad that there have been so many deaths and that there is likely to be many more.

By A'niyah Fenton, aged 9

A'niyah enjoys singing, dancing and helping people. Her hobbies are knitting, playing her recorder and riding her bike. Her favourite book is 'The World's Worst Children' by David Walliams and her favourite film is 'Zootropolis'. A'niyah is a friendly girl – she makes friends with others easily and has lots of friends. A'niyah likes to go on holiday, help with the cooking and she likes school.

Grandad Osa Chris Ikhinmwin

Our grandad is amazing! His name is Orobosa (in Jehovah's hands) Osadolor (Jehovah repairs) Christopher (Christ bearer) Ikhinmwin (solid roots). Most people know him as Chris. He was born on 16 February 1951 in Ogbe Quarters, in Benin City, Nigeria, Africa. His mother's name was Grace Enene and she was a trader of gold and coral beads. His father was Stephen Agho, who was originally a hunter and a farmer but became a chief inspector of police in Nigeria.

Grandad's dad was a very tough man who believed if you were educated you could do anything. His mum was always very kind. When she cooked, she'd keep her front door unlocked so people could walk in and help themselves to the food she cooked. She loved serving people and being kind to others.

Our grandad had lots of siblings because his dad married 12 wives and they each had lots of children. Grandad was the seventh child and grew up in a nice neighbourhood in Benin City. As a child, Grandad would go into the bush to catch bush rats and rabbits to eat. He made his own toys too! One of his favourite toys was a car made from cocoyam leaves, bark, rope and broomsticks. His best friends were his brother George and another boy called Godspower. They went to Eweka Primary School, but Grandad transferred to Okere Primary School after his dad was promoted to head of Warri Police Station.

Once, as a young boy, Grandad was attending an inter-sports event and didn't have money to get home. So, Grandad held onto the tail of a lorry that was taking everyone home. It was a dangerous, bumpy, 40-minute journey. One mistake by the driver and Grandad could have fallen into the road and been killed.

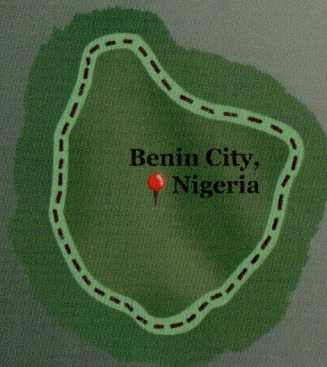

Benin City, Nigeria

When Grandad was 26, his mum died in childbirth. Her death shocked him. He said it's scary when somebody who isn't sick goes into hospital and doesn't come back because they have died.

Following the loss of his mum, he made plans to move to England. He was accepted into Camberwell School of Arts and Crafts but, a month before he was due to travel, his grandad died. They were very close so he stayed for the funeral. In 1978, on 31 October, at the age of 27, Grandad arrived in England. Two years later, Grandad married Grandma. They had grown up together in Nigeria and were very good friends when they were young. One day, he asked her "Is it ok for us to be together?" After some consideration, she said, "Yes." They married and had five children, but one died. Our daddy Samuel is his third child. His name means 'God has heard'. Our grandad's favourite sport is basketball and his favourite athlete is professional basketball player and captain of the London Lions, his son, Joe Ikhinmwin. As a parent, Grandad was very strict on his sons but he became more lenient when they became teenagers. He feels blessed to have 11 grandchildren.

One of Grandad's most memorable moments is the time he saw Michael Jackson when he visited the Queen Elizabeth Hospital for Children in Hackney, London. Grandad is well travelled. He has been to Germany, Italy, Holland, Spain, Austria, Ghana, Turkey and America. His favourite place is Berlin because even with the language barrier, it was a very quiet and peaceful place. In 1988, Grandad's father died in Nigeria, aged 76, due to ill health. Unfortunately, Grandad could not travel back to Nigeria to attend the funeral because the British immigration department at that time said they would not allow him to come back into England if he left.

Grandad's favourite food is yam and owo soup with fish. It's his native soup from Benin City and he thinks it tastes delicious and is healthy. The last time he ate it was back home in Nigeria. He says maybe we could learn to cook it for him! Grandad is happy when he looks at his children and thinks of the grace of Jesus Christ – he is thankful for everything.

Covid-19 has really humbled and shown Grandad that it is only God's grace that keeps us alive. He calls coronavirus the 'Evil Wind'.

By Abigail and Elijah Ikhinmwin, aged 6 and 5

Abigail is a natural born leader: confident, strong-willed and bold. She is an avid reader and is extremely talented at writing and gymnastics. She enjoys reading the Bible and books about science. Elijah enjoys colouring and building things from scratch. He won gold and silver medals in his first two karate competitions. When he is older, he wants to be a chef and a Prophet for God, just like his namesake in the Bible.

Nana Maxine Julie Samuel

My nana's name is Maxine Julie Samuel. She is known as Julie in her family because her older sister is also named Maxene. She was born on 29 May 1962 in Wirksworth, Derby, England. Her mother's name is Rachel Hamilton and she is a retired mental health nurse and her father's name was Emmanuel Hamilton. He was an engineer for National Rail.

My nana's earliest memory is of living in a nice, little, three-bedroom house with a massive garden. She lived with seven of her nine siblings and a dog, so the house was always crowded. The boys shared one room, the girls shared one room and her parents shared the other. She wasn't too keen on the dog because it used to bark at her and her brothers and sisters when they tried to get into the house after school.

Her childhood was fun though – she used to play in the park with her siblings, climb trees, pick apples, and knock on people's doors and then run off (she found this quite funny). My nana and her siblings were always playing outdoors, rarely indoors, although she'd often stay at her best friend's house and they'd watch television together. Her parents didn't buy a television for their house until she was eight years old; it was a black and white television, which was normal back then.

Her childhood was so much fun, but one thing, she didn't enjoy was having to help her dad with the garden and with tidying up. He was very strict, but she would get £1.50 pocket money every week for doing her chores. This was great because it meant she could go to the shop and buy sweets – drumstick squashies are still her favourites! She attended Homelands Secondary School for Girls and then later, when they moved house, Littleover Community School.

Derby, England

My nana never went to college; she left secondary school and went straight into work as a seamstress making deep sea diving suits. To make sure they didn't leak, she tested them in a big bath of water. The faster she worked the more money she could make and she was really quick so she made around £300 a week. Every payday, she'd give some money to her mother and then save the rest.

My nana loves helping people and has had many jobs including: childminder, children's healthcare assistant, mental health assistant, and support worker for adults with learning disabilities. She is now the centre manager for a sensory learning and play centre for children with additional needs.

She has been married for 32 years, has five children and 10 grandchildren. A very big family! Spending time with her family and friends makes her happy. She also enjoys living her life for God and volunteering for the church and community.

The day my nana gave birth to my mum, she went into labour at three o'clock in the morning and was rushed to Royal Derby Hospital by my grandad. But there was a problem – when they reached the hospital, she couldn't get out of the car. My grandad called for a midwife to help them and the midwife told them my mum's head was crowning and that my nana had to give birth where she was; in the car.

My nana loves to go on adventures and explore new countries. She has travelled to Canada, Tunisia, Mexico, USA, Turkey, Spain and Jamaica (where her parents are from). Her favourite holiday destination is Antigua, where my grandad grew up. She even took a road trip one summer with her family to visit as many theme parks as they could in 3 weeks!

She has always been very active – she played netball with her church in Nottingham and took pilates back in Derby. Her favourite athlete is Usain Bolt because he shows commitment and resilience.

My nana thinks that the Covid-19 pandemic is very strange – having to stay at home, not go out to work and wait on the government's advice. She can't wait until it's over because she misses seeing her children and grandchildren. She hopes that, once the pandemic is over, people will value each other more, and especially nurses and carers.

By Amirah Edinborough , aged 8

Amirah is a very bubbly and thoughtful girl who takes pride in being a big sister. She loves exploring the outdoors, swimming, imaginative play with dolls and Lego, and singing in the school choir. She has also recently started learning how to play the guitar, taught by her grandad. At church, Amirah performs with the children flag dancers, sings in the choir and takes part in the children's service where she has grown in confidence to speak publicly in front of a big group of people. Amirah's favourite book is 'The World's Worst Teachers' by David Walliams.

Nanaa Mavis Jones

Mavis Camille Jones, also known as Nanaa-May, was born at home on 29 December 1943 at 23 Gurling Street, Cross Roads, St Andrews in Jamaica. Nanaa's mum was Adeline Anderson and she worked in a children's hospital and her dad was Sylbert Jones who was a lorry driver.

Her mum was loving and caring and always provided for Nanaa, but she didn't know her father very well because he sadly died in a car crash when she was very young. Her grandmother was a housewife and her grandfather worked on a farm all the way in Panama! Nanaa had an elder brother, called Neville, who was three years older than her. She remembers Jamaican life as idyllic, it was the kind of place where you could go out anywhere and leave the door unlocked. It was very safe.

When Nanaa's mum came to England, Nanaa stayed behind with her aunty Irene Cooper. She loved Aunty Irene very much.

Nanaa's school was only five minutes from her house and her best friend Eileen Loague (whose nickname was Peggy) lived nearby too. Little Mavis and Peggy would have lots of fun playing together, climbing trees, building makeshift houses and playing make-believe. When they grew up, Peggy married a German man in London and Nanaa lost touch with her best friend. She has always hoped they will find each other again one day.

Nanaa was a very well-behaved child and her school teacher loved her. Her teacher would often invite her round for tea and she also got to carry the teacher's books at school – an important task reserved only for the best students. When she was young, she knew she wanted to be either a teacher or a postmistress when she grew up. Being a postmistress in Jamaica was seen as a very professional job, plus she just really wanted to wear the cool uniform! In the end, Nanaa's career took a completely different path and she became a nurse.

Nanaa says she has only ever been naughty once. When she was nine years old, she attended the Junkanoo with her mum. The Junkanoo is a popular winter street festival in Jamaica named after the Ghanaian folk hero, John Canoe. People dress up in elaborate costumes, dance and sing, and eat lots of yummy food. While at the festival, Nanaa was mesmerised by one of the parade dancers, wearing a brightly coloured costume, and before she knew it she had followed them into the crowd. She was lost for one whole hour! Nanaa's mum didn't know where she was and she got tapped on her bottom for wandering off.

Nanaa had five children in total. My dad, Derek, was her first child who she said was a lovely baby. He was born on a Wednesday at two o'clock in the morning and, although Nanaa says it was painful, she says he was a joy.

My dad was followed by my aunts and uncles; Rose, Sonia, Junior and Fitzroy. All Nanaa's children were good at drawing, sewing and cooking.

Nanaa didn't join her mother in England until she was 15 years old. When she was 13 years old, her cousin made a lovely turquoise dress for her, which she later wore on the journey to England. She also loves tennis (especially Andy Murray and the Williams sisters), the author, Maya Angelou, the film, 'The Colour Purple' and the country, Cyprus – her favourite holiday destination. Nanaa's favourite song is 'It is Well With my Soul' and she loves reading the Bible too. Her favourite passage from the scripture is from John 3:16, 'For God so loved the world that he gave his only begotten son, that whosoever believeth in him shall not perish but have everlasting life'.

By Anayo Rose-Morrison, aged 8

Anayo loves reading and being read to by his mum, he also loves playing Roblox with his brother Kayin. His favourite book is a book he wrote called 'Something' – it is very funny. His best holiday was in Greece because there was a swimming pool and a play area and he got to stay up till late. He loves to swim and has achieved stage 4 in swimming. He also likes karate and playing piano.

Nana Persis Jackson

My grandmother's name is Persis Jackson. Everyone called her Peenie after 'peenie wallies' (the name given to fireflies in Jamaica) because she had bright eyes. She was born at home in Jamaica in a place called St Catherine on 17 November 1936 – the third child out of five brothers and three sisters. Her mother was Letitia Jackson, a dedicated housewife, and her father was Ferdinand Jackson, a bus driver.

St Catherine is a parish that grew plenty of crops and fruits. Nana's favourite East Indian mango grew in abundance everywhere. She would just pick them from the trees in her garden and sometimes, as school kids, they would cheekily throw stones at other people's mango trees so the fruit would fall and they could eat them. Each morning, Nana would wake up and collect water from the spring with her donkey, Sammy. He was quiet and easy going.

Children were expected to help out at home so she would make breakfast for the family; eggs from her hens, callaloo and saltfish. They didn't have lots of money but they were very happy. Nana's close relatives lived nearby. Aunty Jenny had long, beautiful hair that she would use to help her carry a pan of water on her head. Uncle Massa was a tall, handsome farmer who raised animals for sale and Nana's grandmother, Isobella, would plait Nana's hair every morning. They called Isobella 'Mammy'. She was great at preparing cured smoked meats that Nana loved to eat.

As a child, Nana loved playing with her dog, Rover, but skipping and hopscotch were her favourite. Nana and her friends would use chalk to draw the squares wherever they could. They also played a game called moonshine baby: at night you'd lie on the ground, a friend would use stones and broken pottery to make an outline of your body and you had to try and get up without moving the outline. Nana's best friend was a girl, called Curline Bogle, who was clever and beautiful. Curline moved to Canada and sadly, they lost contact with each other.

Graduating from Jericho Secondary School and Villmore School of Commerce. Nana learned how to do shorthand typing and some bookkeeping. However, Nana really wanted to be a nurse and, eventually came to England where she got married, had children, and achieved her nursing dream.

Nana is one of the Windrush Generation, who were invited to come to Britain to help build up the country. It was a difficult time as Nana and her family had to adjust to a new life in a country where there was a lot of racism. However, the community stuck together and helped each other out. They developed a saving and borrowing scheme called 'pardner' because the banks refused to lend them money. Although things were hard, there were many parties where the community would get together and have fun. Despite being a nurse, my nana had a secret passion: she loved singing. In the 1970s, she recorded her version of a song, 'Since I Met You, Baby'.

Nana remembers the day that my brother, Jacob, was born because it was very dramatic. Mum had become very sick with a syndrome that shut down her major organs. Nana thought my mum may not make it through, but Nana and the family prayed for my mum and she made a full recovery. When my mum had me in hospital, Nana was worried that the same thing would happen again, but it didn't. She thanks God for his mercy and healing grace.

Cricket and tennis are Nana's favourite sports. She remembers when the West Indies were the best team in the world at cricket and she still enjoys watching them beat other teams. Jamaica is her favourite place to visit and Nana believes Jamaica has the best food, beaches and people in the world. Nana also loves reggae, country music, and rhythm and blues. Basically, anything with a good beat.

Covid-19 has taught my nana that everything and anything can be taken away from you without any warning. She says, "Everyone must do their best to enjoy the life they have, as tomorrow is not guaranteed."

By Ava-Marie Udeh, aged 6

Ava-Marie is a happy, loving child, who is always concerned about helping others. She is incredibly inquisitive and is always asking questions about the world around her. Ava-Marie is a keen gymnast and thoroughly enjoys rolling and tumbling everywhere. She has a passion for cooking and can be regularly seen in the kitchen helping her nana. Her favourite book is 'Amazing Grace' by Mary Hoffman because nothing stopped Grace from achieving her dreams.

Grandad Gladstone Dennis

Born on 1 June 1952 in Savanna la Mar, Westmoreland, Jamaica, my grandad Gladstone Dennis was the son of a cleaner called Elfreda and a labourer named Stanford. He was the youngest of six brothers and they all lived on top of a hill. In their backyard were wildlife and plants, like sugar cane and mango trees, and animals, like chickens and pigs. He even had a pet donkey, which he used to ride as a child.

Grandad has fond memories of fishing trips with his family – it was tradition that any fish they caught during the day would be brought back home and cooked by his mother for supper. A dish of yam, dumplings, green banana and fish has always been his favourite meal. Grandad's chores were very different to mine; he'd fetch water, get yams from the ground and feed the donkey, the pigs and the chickens.

There was one chicken in particular which was his favourite. One day, Grandad came home for dinner and his mother had made him chicken, dumplings and yam. He was very hungry so he gobbled it up and found it really tasty. Later on, he was searching the yard for his pet chicken, but couldn't find him anywhere. His brothers, laughing, told him he had eaten his pet chicken for dinner and Grandad was so upset he cried himself to sleep.

To entertain themselves, my grandad and his brothers would make their own toys, which included slingshots for bird hunting games and wooden swords for play fighting. But his most favourite toy was called a 'gig' – a makeshift spinning top, created using a round piece of wood that would spin off a nail stuck through its middle. If you had the best gig in the area, other children would challenge you – the last gig standing wins. My grandad loved the game!

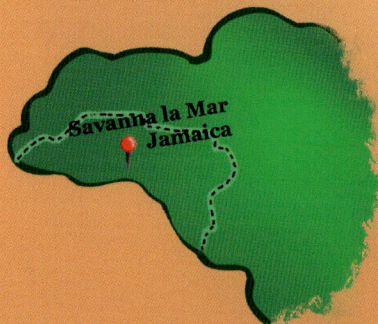

When Grandad lived in Jamaica, he attended a primary school in Williamsfield, but he moved to England where he started secondary school when he was 13 years old. His cousin went to the same school, so he had some company.

Savanna la Mar
Jamaica

It must have been hard starting a new school – especially one in a completely new country. Grandad and his cousin stayed close throughout school and they are still best friends over fifty years later!

As a child, Grandad loved to read; particularly fictional books based on true stories. He always had a dictionary on hand to look up the meanings of words he didn't know so that he could expand his vocabulary. He says, "Words are power!" Grandad was clever at school and he worked hard. He didn't like history very much because they never taught the role of black people in British history, but he loved science. He always hoped that one day he could be a doctor and help to take care of sick people. The best way for him to make this happen would be to join the army and become a doctor that way. However, my great-grandparents, Elfreda and Stanford, refused to sign the papers allowing him to enlist, which meant he couldn't join. Looking back now, he says he's happy they said no. Grandad's first job was an apprenticeship to be a sheet metalworker, but when he looked at the workers and saw that they were in poor shape due to bending over to hammer metal every day, he asked the manager if he could try something else. Next, he tried welding. But he wasn't happy with that either as the pay was very low. He tried many different jobs after this, concluding that the metal business wasn't for him.

Grandad remembers buying his very first car, a grey Ford Corsair. Although the car was his, he had to be driven around in it by friends because, at the time, he couldn't legally drive. He met my grandma at a disco club and they got married in the lounge of a public house in front of 50 guests. They had four children.

Grandad doesn't like to think much about Covid-19 as he is uncertain what it all means but he says we should all stay at home and keep safe.

By Cleo Dennis, aged 13

Cleo is a child of Jamaican descent who enjoys writing poetry, singing and playing badminton. Her favourite book is 'Boys Don't Cry' by her favourite author, Malorie Blackman. And her favourite film is 'Spirited Away'. She enjoys eating jollof rice and banana fritters with her Nigerian and Jamaican friends from her grammar school.

Grandad Geeroy Jackson

My grandad's name is Geeroy Jackson. He was born in Bartons, St Catherine, Jamaica in 1960. His mother, Olga Jackson, was a housewife and his father, Kenneth Jackson, worked in a factory as a plant charger.

My grandad was the fifth child of eight children. He lived with his grandmother in one big family home. They didn't go on family trips, but everyone was always together and his neighbourhood community was fantastic because they shared crops and goods. Grandad says the most important lesson his parents taught him was that family matters. His favourite drink is sugar water mixed with orange. It is something they used to drink back home while they were at the river as it was refreshing during the hot, sunny days. The first time he saw a television was in 1967 in Freetown, Jamaica – he watched 'Bonanza', a popular western movie.

While in Jamaica, my grandad admittedly was a bit of a troublemaker and found it hard to settle, so he moved school quite a lot. When he turned 12, his parents sent for him to join them and his younger sibling in the UK, at their new home in, Kensal Green, North West London.

My great-grandfather, Kenneth, always looked after his children and taught them how to look after themselves properly. This meant my grandad had to learn how to do a lot of chores. He'd tidy the beds, clean the oven; basically, clean the whole house! He didn't get any pocket money either because the family only had enough money for food. Life at my grandad's new home in the UK was great because all the kids on the street played together. They played cricket and flew kites. He had learnt how to make top quality handmade kites back home in Jamaica; these were the best! Whilst his friend's shop-bought kites soon fell to the ground, my grandad's kite could go on flying for hours and hours.

St. Catherine
Jamaica

When my grandad was 13, his family moved to Greenford, where he attended a grammar school. He was a smart pupil and achieved top grades, but sadly the school was closed down after his first year there.

He had no choice but to move to the local public school, which was a terrible thing because that was where he experienced a lot of racism. He wanted to become a printer – designing photographs, newspapers and magazines, but he was told it wasn't for his 'kind'. You had to know someone in the business to get in, which was the same for a lot of jobs at that time – this made it especially difficult for black families that had moved to the UK not knowing anybody.

My grandparents met in college and my father was born when my grandad was in his early twenties. He named him Geeroy, after himself, as he felt it was a special name. Later, Grandad got married in Barbados in front of 33 guests and had two more children; Alexandra and Georgina. He always encouraged his children to fulfil their dreams. He worked very hard to get a high-profile job, which allowed him to travel to over 30 countries all around the world, spending a long period of time in Australia, but his favourite place to travel to was Senegal.

I asked Grandad what his favourite thing is about being a grandparent and he laughed, joking "I can hand the kids back at the end of the day." He's always had a fun sense of humour. He's really active too! He trained professionally in martial arts and has competed in competitions and he's a personal trainer.

We were in lockdown for a long time and now some people are returning to work – my grandad tells me that when he goes to work, he has to have his temperature checked before he can enter. My grandad thinks that the information about Covid-19 has not been laid out to us clearly and he is not happy about what the government has to say about it. They also haven't told us the difference between a common cold and the coronavirus – he says people need clarity!

By Courtney Jackson, aged 8

Courtney loves to perform and attends Stagecoach Performing Arts where she does dance, drama and singing. She's also very active and takes part in track athletic competitions – she's very fast and has even won a gold medal. Courtney's favourite movie is 'Four Kids and It' based on the book, 'Four Children and It' by Jacqueline Wilson. Her favourite book series is 'Dork Diaries'.

Granny Cheryl Hernandez

My granny's name is Cheryl Hernandez. She was born on 6 November 1950 in Woodbrook, Port of Spain, Trinidad. Her mum was Yvonne Joyce Woodroffe, a senior accountant for the government, and her father was Louis Anthony Woodroffe, a public servant. Granny lived in Louis Street, La Puerta Avenue, Diego Martin.

Her maternal grandparents were Clementina and Hubert Charles. Granny knew Clementina the best. She was a housewife who never worked but had excellent money management skills. Hubert was a carpenter with his own furniture shop. He also bought, renovated and re-sold properties for a profit. Her paternal grandfather, Horatio Woodroffe, owned estate lands and used to farm and sell cocoa. He lived in a modest, little home called 'Cocoa House' where the roof could slide out and expose the ceiling. To grind up the cocoa, they'd put all the seeds on top of the ceiling and Granny remembers going to the estate and seeing people dance on the slide out roof, grinding up all the cocoa.

Granny was the first-born child and had two younger brothers called Louis and Gordon, and their father raised two goats in the backyard from which they got their milk. She loved cricket and all the neighbourhood kids would get together and play in the streets.

When she was younger, Granny learned how to sew her own clothes – she's really good at it! Once, when she was home alone, she was sewing together a new outfit for herself when she heard footsteps coming up the stairs. It was a thief! Granny screamed as loud as she could and the neighbours heard and called the police.

Port of Spain, Trinidad

Granny's dad had an old car called an Austin Devon that he used to take the children to school. Then there was a neighbour called Mr Rivers who had no car and always wanted a free ride. Mr Rivers would time when Granny and Great-grandpa would leave the house so he could catch a lift. Granny didn't like this at all because whenever Mr Rivers got in the car, the pleats in her dress got crushed. So, she asked her brother to put a pin where Mr Rivers normally sits. The next day, the car wouldn't start.

Mr Rivers decided he couldn't wait all day and left. When the car finally started, her brother forgot about the pin and sat on it. "OOOOOOWWWWWW!" he screamed. When their dad asked what had happened, her brother sold her out and granny got spanked for being selfish and unkind.

Once, when Granny was driving her car, another car bashed into her side. She wasn't hurt, but she was so shocked by what happened that when she drove into the nearby university car park, she didn't press on her brake. She just kept driving and heading straight into the direction of the university building. One of the guards at the entrance had to run alongside the car and shout to get her attention, so that she would stop driving.

In 2007 when Granny was in England, Doctor S diagnosed Granny with stage 3 cancer. The doctor had to operate on Granny. It was a very scary time for Granny and the family. After the operation Granny got better very quickly. We are all happy that Granny is still alive with us today and is able to visit us every summer.

Granny really enjoys travelling. She's been to Liverpool with us, which was lots of fun and she has been to Chicago, Miami, New York and Canada. She also went on a Mediterranean cruise for her sixtieth birthday and visited Monaco, Italy and Spain. Her favourite athlete is Hasely Crawford, Trinidad's first Olympic gold medallist. Her favourite sweets are donuts and pineapple cake and her favourite ice cream flavour is coconut – I've never tried that flavour before.

My granny believes that Covid-19 was manmade and backfired on the inventors. She also feels that it's a good opportunity for the world to heal.

By Diego Ross, aged 9

Diego loves to read and write comics. His favourite books are the 'Mr Gum' series by Andy Stanton and he's currently reading the 'Smartboys Club Series' by Rebecca Shelley. Diego has been swimming and doing judo for almost 3 years and he won a trophy in his first year for 'Best Newcomer, runner up'. Diego's mum is from Trinidad & Tobago and his Dad is from England. He considers himself mixed race because between his parents he has Nigerian, Ghanaian (by way of the Caribbean), Native American (most likely Warao), Scottish, English, Irish, French and German, Spanish and Scandinavian heritage.

Grandad Nick Amaechi Udeh

My grandfather's name is Nick Amaechi Udeh. Our family is from Egede village in Engu State, Nigeria, but he was born in Port Harcourt, Nigeria. He is the eldest of seven children – he has two brothers and four sisters. They grew up in Port Harcourt up until the Biafran War in 1967. His mother was Catherine Afiaugbo Udeh, a housewife, and his father was Patrick Udegbuman Udeh, a railway worker.

His earliest childhood memory was of my great-grandmother pleading with the local primary school to allow my grandad to start school because he was very active and restless at home. Back then, they did a quick test on children to decide whether they were old enough to start school. They would ask you to put your right arm over your head to see if you could touch the tip of your left ear. My grandad couldn't do it, but they accepted him because of my great-grandmother's persuasion.

My grandad had to change schools when the family moved to a bigger house. His school was three miles away from the house and my grandad had to walk there and back every day for a whole year. He used chalk and slate to learn in school, and sticks, cardboard and other materials to create toys. He loved music and played the cymbal in the school band. He later moved up to playing the drums. The bandmaster was very impressed with him when he discovered that he could play the drums very well. He was the smallest person in the school band, the drums were much bigger than him but it helped to make him popular in school – he was known as 'the small boy who played the large drums very well'.

Enugu
Nigeria

Grandad was very active in the church too and loved to sing. When he was younger, he was an altar boy and in the choir. At college, he formed a pop band with his friends – 'The Beach Boys' – because his college was by the seaside. The pop band was so good that a regional television station invited them to perform live on television.

But it was when the Nigeria-Biafran War broke out that things changed. Many families became refugees.

26

My grandad joined the Biafran Army when where he lived was under threat. He was only 21 years old. There was a lot of hunger and sickness, so to ensure the safety of his family and other families, he arranged for a large truck to move them from their village to a place behind enemy lines that was safer.

Grandad fought on the frontline for over a year, where he saw so many horrible things he will never forget. He sadly lost his much-loved classmate, John Nzekwe, who was shot dead during the war. Grandad also worked as an undercover military agent, going on secret missions to identify people who may have been a threat to the army.

Once the war ended in 1970, Grandad started afresh. He struggled on his own for some time until he got a job at Central Bank of Nigeria when he was 24 years old.

After years of working hard and sending money to his parents to help them with food and school fees for his siblings, Grandad married my grandma, which he said is the best thing he has ever done. She was very patient and kind. They travelled to the UK as Grandad got a scholarship to study finance and accounting. By this time, Grandad had two children: my Dad, Melvin, and Uncle Frank.

Due to the foreign exchange restrictions in place he had difficulties receiving money in the UK from Nigeria. He decided to sacrifice his scholarship so that he could earn money whilst studying to support and look after his family. My Grandad, throughout his life, has been a hardworking businessman.

Grandad says life is much easier now than it was for him growing up. He advises all young people today to take advantage of everything they can. He says, "There is so much opportunity now. The future is yours for the taking."

By Jacob Udeh, aged 9

Jacob is a kind boy who has a passion for football. He is often found in the garden practising and perfecting his footballing skills. At the tender age of seven years old, Jacob published his first children's story: 'Jacob's day trip to Jamaica'. He is keen to build on this success and create a prolific legacy as a young black writer whose stories connect with young black children everywhere.

Grandad Franklyn Ocarriell McNeilly

My grandad's name is Franklyn Ocarriell McNeilly. He also goes by the names OC and Okro, which are shortened versions of his middle name. Many people in Grenada are given nicknames by people in the village and are rarely referred to as their birth name. My grandad was born on 15 October 1963. However, his birth certificate says that he was born on 16 October 1963 because his mother registered him a day late. His mother, my late great-grandmother, gave birth to him in their family home in River Sallee, St Patrick's, Grenada. My grandad's mum's name was Catherine McNeilly and she was a care worker. His father's name was Raymond McNeilly and he was a builder.

My grandad is the fifth of nine children. His siblings' names are Ashton, Ronnie, Ann, Johanna, Ralph, Katy, Nadine and Nelliann. What my grandad remembers most about his childhood was that he used to get teased for having misplaced teeth. Children would sometimes tease him and say he had 'pack pack teeth'. He laughs at this now, but he didn't find it funny at all back then. River Sallee was a nice place to live, Grandad had fresh air, happy neighbours and beautiful beaches. It was a really friendly neighbourhood to grow up in. His best friend growing up was his cousin, Randolph. He says they grew up as close as brothers. As a child, he would mainly play with the farm animals, such as the goats and sheep. However, his favourite pet was his rabbit.

Once, when my grandad was a child, he climbed up on his mum's expensive cabinet, causing it to fall down and all of the glass shattered. Knowing that he would get into trouble, Grandad rushed to bed early and pretended to sleep. A little while later, his mum called him downstairs to get a beating and instead of pretending to be asleep, he forgot, and shouted back, "Mummy, I'm sleeping!" The whole family started laughing.

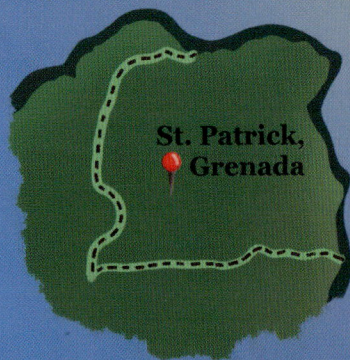

St. Patrick, Grenada

My grandad has had many jobs in his life such as being a farmer, tailor, builder and property developer. He was off sick from work due to a severe accident whilst working on a roof. He has been self-employed for the majority of his working life and has always encouraged his children and grandchildren to work for themselves and to become self-sufficient. His dream is to retire and return to Grenada.

My grandad met my nana in 1988 during a church service, when she was on holiday in Carriacou, which is an island off mainland Grenada. My nana's name is Deborah but I call her 'Mummy Nana'. She was born in Carriacou and was visiting her friends and family at the time of meeting my grandad. My grandad and nana later went on to get married in 1989 and had three daughters together.

Their eldest child is my mum, Nerissa. Their second child is my aunty Alisha and their third child is my aunty Rhianna. My nana is very loving and caring and has always been there for me since I was a baby. My nana is a nurse and she loves her job because she is passionate about caring for people in need. The biggest lesson my nana has taught me is to always be respectful to others. My nana thoroughly enjoys spending time with her family and is usually the one who initiates family days out and family movie nights. I go to visit her sometimes after school and at the weekends and she makes the best mac and cheese! When it's time to leave my nana's house to go back home, I often look outside my mum's rear car window and see my nana standing outside the front door with a big smile on her face waving us goodbye as we drive away.

My grandad enjoys watching sports. His favourite sports stars are Muhammed Ali, the boxer, and Brian Lara, the cricketer. They are both considered to be world champions in their sport. Out of everyone who has ever lived, the person, Grandad finds the most inspiring, is Malcom X as he took a powerful stand for the rights of black people. Grandad's first car was an Austin 120Y. He loves rice and peas, John 3:16 is his favourite bible verse and he loves soul music – anything with a bit of rhythm.

My grandad believes that Covid-19 is a man-made virus. However, on a spiritual level, he also believes it is a prophecy from the Bible that is manifesting. He describes the global pandemic we are currently in as 'very tragic'.

By Jamil McNeilly, aged 11

Jamil enjoys learning and his favourite subject at school is science as he has a particular interest in human biology. Jamil aspires to become a surgeon when he is older. He loves sport, especially table tennis, hockey, football and basketball. His favourite movies are comedies such as 'White Chicks' and 'Little Man', but he also enjoys action and thriller movies. His favourite genres of books and movies are Japanese anime and fantasy fiction. He has recently discovered a passion for writing and wants to be a part of a project that gives back to the community.

Grandad Vincent Augustus Lewis

My grandad's name is Vincent Augustus Lewis, aka Shorty because he was short and he was the smallest twin. He and his brother were born on 12 March 1952 in Santa Cruz, St Elizabeth Parish in Jamaica. His mother was Ina Lewis and she was a transport worker for London Underground. His father was Vernon Lewis and a health inspector. His parents were hardworking people, who took great care of their family.

Grandad and his twin brother, Vivian Lewis, (aka Bigga) were born prematurely and had to be delivered at the family home. Grandad was so small they had to tie him to a pillow – they didn't have incubators in those days. His grandma, Gong Gong, lived in the family home and she used to take care of him, bathe him and comb his hair. She was a very caring woman and would wipe his tears if he fell down. When Grandad was a child, he liked to cycle, play cricket, ride horses and his pet donkey. For his chores, he used to help his grandma and mum feed and tend to the cattle and goats.

In 1963, when he was 11 years old, he came to England and settled in Wood Green, North London. He remembers how cold it was, and that everyone in the area knew each other. It was also the first time he saw a television. Grandad loved learning about the world even back when he was a child. After coming to England, he read the book 'Roots' by Alex Haley and it taught him a lot about history and culture. Back in Jamaica, the history of slavery was never taught to him so, when he came to England, he learned all about it himself. He didn't like swimming though – he still doesn't. Living far from the sea in Jamaica, he'd never learned how to swim; so swimming in a pool in cold England wasn't fun.

Grandad passed his driving test in 1970 when he was 18 years old and his first car was a Vauxhall Astra. He says driving was better back in the day and he does not like to drive now because there is always traffic and nowhere to park. My grandad loves horses – he always wanted to be a famous race jockey and go to Cheltenham when he grew up. Instead he got his first job as an engineer's apprentice and got paid £20 a week.

St. Elizabeth
Jamaica

Family is very important to my grandad. He has only been married once, to my grandmother. They got married in Wood Green with a reception in Tottenham and it was grand – they looked like a king and queen in front of 150 guests. Grandad says no other woman can walk in her shoes. She was the love of his life and he believes if everyone was like her the world would be a much better place. His twin brother passed away in 1984. Even though they were not identical twins, Grandad and Great-uncle Vivian shared a special connection. They did everything together, they went to church together, they worked together and they had so much fun. Grandad says he will never forget him.

Grandad is proud of being Jamaican. Jamaica is his favourite place in the whole world. His favourite artist is Bob Marley, the king of reggae music and he loves all his songs – he even met him once! Grandad says everyone in the world knows about Bob Marley and his music will live forever because he is a legend. Grandad also likes art – his favourite painting is of the Queen of Sheba. History and geography were his favourite subjects at school and he still enjoys them to this day because he says it's good to know about the world and your history.

My grandad says the Covid-19 crisis is a world disaster. He believes the government do not have any sense and that we have to take care of each other. He also said it's going to be PMH – that means Poverty, Murder and Hunger.

By Kalisha Shor-Maxam, aged 9

Kalisha is a bright, compassionate child who loves her family and the Arts. She attends Storm the Stage Academy of Arts (STS) where she participates in afro fusion, contemporary and acrobatic dancing – her favourite style is afro dancing. Kalisha spends many hours choreographing her own dances and has represented her school at national level where her team gained first and second place in different categories. She has also attended the New London Performing Arts Centre where she has participated in many roles; her favourite was 'Annie' where she played the lead character. Her favourite book is currently 'No Dinner for Anansi' by Emma Shaw-Smith and Trish Cooke.

Grandad James Uriah Rose

My grandad's name is James Uriah Rose. Some people call him Jimmy Rose and he was born at home in Hatfield, Jamaica on 19 April 1933. That was his official date of birth but his dad who was given the details to register him did not do this until 28 May 1933 so that's the date on his birth certificate. His father, Joseph Theophilus Rose, was a farmer and his mother, Agnes Eliza Rose, was a housewife.   Before she was married, everybody would call her Miss Berry. Grandad called his grandparents Moomah and Poopah. They had a very large property called Dunsenhale where they grew a spice called pimento that was sold and shipped to England.

Grandad's mum, Eliza, had seven children. His sister, Iris, died when she was three months old and his older brother, Adrian, died at the age of 15. James Uriah Rose, my grandad, was the youngest child and he grew up with sisters Beryl and Ruby who were older than him. His mum, Eliza, also had two children outside of marriage, Victor and Doris, who lived with their grandparents.

When my grandad was little, Poopah used to buy beef from Mr Borah, the butcher in Mandeville and Moomah would teach Grandad how to cook the beef with rice and peas. Grandad spent a lot of time playing in the fields, eating wild berries, oranges and tangerines – there was a lot of fruit at home in Jamaica. The children all went to school in the week, and on Saturday, they cleaned the house and looked after the animals. On Sunday, they went to church and did their homework. For fun they used to play chevy chase. The rule for chevy chase was if someone taps you, you're out the game. The elders didn't want grandad or his friends to play marbles because they thought if they did, the children would become gamblers. When he was young, Grandad wanted to be a train driver when he grew up. There was only one train that ran through his area from Williams Field to Montego Bay.

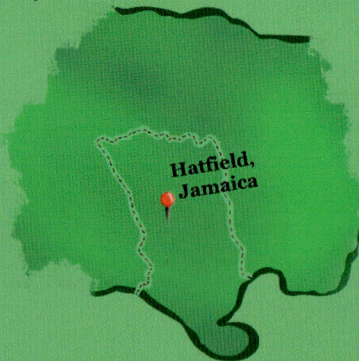

Hatfield,
Jamaica

When Grandad came to the UK it was so different from Jamaica; the cold, the snow, the food, the housing. The cold was a shock. Grandad was lucky because he had a trade as a carpenter so he got work easily.

My grandad shared a secret with me that he had never told anyone. One morning, Grandad was late for work and the other men were exiting the changing room having put on their work clothes. When Grandad got to the changing room, he saw someone had left some money on the bench: seven pounds and ten shillings (a lot of money in those days). Grandad picked up the money and told a colleague he was going to return it to the owner. His colleague convinced him to share it with him as they didn't have much money and the owner probably didn't need it or he wouldn't have left it lying around. At the end of the day when they were leaving, Grandad found out that the money belonged to a man who couldn't get home that day or pay his rent. Grandad felt awful. He went back to his colleague and pleaded with him to give back the money, but the colleague refused. Grandad said that, to this day, he regrets ever taking the money. He always hoped that he would come across the gentleman so he could apologise, but he never saw him again. Grandad said this incident has haunted him ever since.

The thing Grandad Rose is most thankful for is meeting his wife Laurel Veronica Rose. Grandad first met my grandma at a church service in Jamaica. When he came to England, they met up again and he proposed over dinner in a restaurant in Lewisham. They had a long courtship because Grandma was studying to be a nurse. Grandma was studying at Joyce Green Nursing College and he would visit her there regularly. His best friend was Roy Smith, who was his next-door neighbour in Jamaica, and after 40 years of not seeing each other they met again in England and now live 20 minutes apart.

Religion keeps my grandad focused and always reminds him that God is always there. A major challenge to his faith was the unlawful killing of his son Winston Rose in police custody in 1981. He doesn't know how he would have dealt with this without God in his life.

Grandad believes that Covid-19 is a sign from God. A sign that God is coming.

By Kayin Rose-Morrison, aged 11

Kayin loves to play drums every Saturday at music school, He is a blue belt in karate and a stage 7 swimmer. In his spare time, Kayin rides his bike and plays football. He loves spending time with his dad watching lots of movies and likes going on adventures with his mum.

Grandad Fitzroy Findlater

My grandfather's name is Fitzroy Carlton Findlater. He is also known as Daddy Mac – everyone calls him that. He was born on 21 January 1957 in England, London, in Alexandra Palace in a bush. His mother was Yvonne Margarita Findlater, a traffic warden, and his father was Joseph Radcliff Findlater, a mechanic. His mum always told him if there was one thing he should learn in life, it's how to cook, wash and iron. His dad was a very quiet man but when he did speak, he was full of wisdom. In his family, there were just two children, Grandad and his brother, Patrick Donavan Findlater, who are five years apart. They grew up in Highbury, which Grandad liked, as everyone got on.

As a child, Grandad would often play King of the castle – one kid would stand on a barrel as 'King' and the other kids would try and take his place. But on one particular day, he was really hungry so went home to eat instead. While he was home, he heard a big bang, followed shortly after by the sound of fire engines. When they heard the fire engines, everyone ran outside to see what was happening. It turns out that one of the kids had lit a match, the barrel blew up and five children died. Grandad was really lucky not to be one of them.

> "His mum always told him if there was one thing he should learn in life, it's how to cook, wash and iron"

Grandad went to Highbury Quadrant Primary School then Highbury Grove Secondary School. He and his friends were very mischievous. My favourite story from Grandad was that in secondary school they used to play a game called left pocket – you would go around and say "left pocket" to someone and the contents of that pocket would automatically belong to you. Those were the rules.

34

Grandad was smart and only kept old tissues in his left pocket, anything important would go in his right pocket, but one time a boy had his mum's rent money in his left pocket and he pleaded with Grandad not to take it, offering instead any item at his house that was of the same value. So, Grandad went to the boy's house and selected a pair of trainers, football boots and a tennis racket – that racket was the start of my grandad's love for the sport. Grandad knew left pocket was a terrible game, but everyone played it and everyone had to follow the rules.

Once he finished school, Grandad did an apprenticeship in mechanics but it wasn't for him – he earned £21 a week and £4.02 was taken in tax. After that, he worked at Moss Bros, a tailoring firm, making coats like the ones fox-hunters wear, then he worked in a shoe factory in Dalston, and then a record factory where they press records. He has had lots of different jobs because it was very easy to change jobs back in the day.

As a parent, Grandad never beat his kids. He just gave them 'the look' and his kids would fall in line. Grandad knew what it was like to get a beating and didn't want that for his children. He says only once was his beating justified – he stole £5 from his mum's purse. That's why now when someone asks him to go into their bag for something, he always takes the bag to them – he never looks into it, himself.

Grandad doesn't like flowers at all – he jokes that maybe it's because he was born in a bush. He's not a fan of board games either – especially not Snakes and Ladders! He used to play it with my mum when she was little and at first, he'd always be in the lead but whenever he got close to winning, he'd land on a really long snake and slide all the way back down to the beginning. Ever since then, he says board games are not his friends.

My grandad says Covid-19 isn't nice at all, especially as he's had close friends who have lost relatives. He's still been going to work, he goes from 6am and is back home at 11am. He says, "The place is a ghost town, not a person or a cat in sight. Very strange times."

By Kaylia Dusauzay, aged 13

Kaylia likes doing nails and is interested in fashion. Her favourite movie is 'It' and she loves to cook for her family. Kaylia is a child model and actress and has appeared in catalogues and in television commercials.

Grandad Desmond Lloyd

St. Ann's Bay
Jamaica

My grandad's name is Desmond Lloyd. He also goes by the nickname Tightman as an endearing term from his peers because he often wore tight trousers as a child. He was born on 31 July 1949 in Saint Ann's Bay, Jamaica. His father, Copeland Lloyd, was a mechanic and his mother, Lurlene (Brown) Lloyd, was a nurse.

My grandad was the fourth of six siblings. He was born at home and not in a hospital which is quite normal in the Caribbean. His first home was in Jamaica and there were lots of fruit trees in their garden like ackee, breadfruit and mango trees. The children would all enjoy climbing those trees. It was fun growing up in Jamaica in the sunshine for my grandad, especially when he would play on the beach, play in the forest, go fishing, play hide and seek, look for fruits or do 100 metre sprints with the other children.

> "he would play on the beach, play in the forest, go fishing, play hide and seek, look for fruits or do 100 metre sprints with the other children."

For pocket money, Grandad used to get two shillings and six pence. He'd use it to buy a nice hot patty, a bit of bread and butter and some grape juice – his favourite! He didn't have many chores either. He'd help his grandma with the shopping but that wasn't really a chore to him because he enjoyed helping her. He used to have an aunty who would give him 10 shillings every time she saw him – that was a lot of money to give a kid in those days.

Grandad really didn't want to come to England when he was a child because he loved Jamaica so much! He was asked to come to England several times, but he managed to delay travelling until after the celebrations on the island following Jamaican independence from British rule. He finally took the trip over in 1962.

Grandad grew up in Kilburn, North West London. He remembers the neighbourhood being okay, he'd play football with the local children but it was nothing like being back home in Jamaica.

Grandad's first adult job was assembling and building electronic apparatus for medical research and for the armed forces. His next job was as an electrician based in Muswell Hill. He'd wire equipment for the Royal Air Force and he'd earn £5 a week. He had many more jobs after that, including driving trains on the London Underground. I love riding the train! Grandad says that the tunnels are all dirty with soot! The longest job he had was with British Telecom as a telephone engineer and that lasted for 15 years. In the 1970s, my grandad enjoyed going to clubs and dancing. One time, my grandad and his friends were filmed by a television crew while dancing in the Apollo Nightclub in north London.

My grandad met my grandma, Norma, when they were children in Jamaica, on a rainy day on the way to church. They had found a parrot and took it home and kept it as a pet for a while before eventually letting it go. In England, as adults, in 1979, they got married and in the same year, my daddy was born. It was around one o'clock in the morning and the first time that Grandad had ever seen a baby born in his life. Now, as a grandparent, my grandad enjoys reading books to me and enjoys taking me out on day trips for bike rides or on the buses and trains. My grandad's favourite holiday was to Tampa in Florida. He went with my grandma, and my daddy and my Auntie Lisa when they were children. They all went to Disney World, ate out at restaurants, went on rides and went to a Ziggy Marley concert!

I asked my grandad about his thoughts on Covid-19 and he was a little sad about it. He thinks that it may not go away for a long while and we will have to get used to a new way of life just like after September 11 2001 when the world changed after the terrorist attack in America.

By Lewis Lloyd, aged 7

Lewis is an intelligent, bright, curious boy, who is quite introverted and a deep thinker. He enjoys learning about maps, transport, astronomy and nature. His favourite genre of books is non-fiction. He achieved an award in school last year for his consistently high-level maths work.

Grandma Mary Williams

My grandma's name is Mary. She is also known as May May because it sounded nice. She was born on 10 July 1941 at home in Delices, Dominica.

Her mother's name was Geraldine and she was a dressmaker and her father's name was Walton and he was a farmer. They were hard workers and planted, grew and sold their food at the local market. Her grandparents were also farmers. Her grandmother Julia was very strong and Mary did not know her grandfather because he had died before she was born.

My grandma grew up on the farm with her five brothers and sisters. She is the third child of six siblings and the only one living in the UK.

Grandma had a happy childhood with loving parents. As a child, her chores included weeding and planting then going to the river to wash clothes and then cook. She had two dogs called Rover and Brackets. She loved playing rum dance, which is a game like rounders, and cricket with the children in the neighbourhood. Grandma would also play with ropes, sticks, balls and marbles because she never had many toys as a child.

Grandma grew up in Delices. Her best friend was a girl who had the same name as Grandma, Mary, and they went to their beloved school together. It was a school for all ages. Grandma was a very clever child and she was in the top class. She loved to read but did not have any books at home; all her reading was through books at school. She told me that if she didn't achieve in her lessons, she would have to go to another school. This made her value education more and to this day she believes there is no excuse not to do and be your best. She has told her children and grandchildren: "Listen to the teachers and if you don't understand, ask the teacher to explain it. If anyone troubles you, you should always tell a teacher."

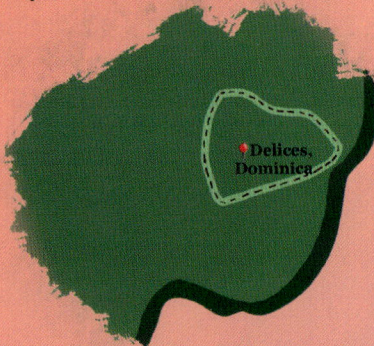

The most stressful experience Grandma has lived through was her journey to England in 1966. When she arrived in London everything seemed so strange and she was frightened. She told me that was the first time she saw a radio and a black and white television. Grandma loved children and wanted to work in a nursery.

When my grandad Francis Williams came to England, he wrote my Grandma a letter asking her if she would be his wife. Grandma was shocked. His family and friends suggested that he would make a good husband and with encouragement from her mum and his mother she decided to make a life with Grandad and they got married on 28 May 1966. They had three children: Desmond, Diane and my daddy, Davis, who was the youngest.

Grandma's favourite sport is horse racing and her favourite painting is a self-portrait that I drew for her. It is on her fridge.

She said that being a grandparent is an honour and a gift from God. What makes my Grandma happy is when she sees her grandchildren, Zach, Makaylah and me, Makai. Her favourite song is 'Here I Am, Lord' and her favourite saying is 'walk with me, oh God, through the darkness, light and brightness'. She is most thankful to God for her health and strength, and for allowing her to be in England for 54 years, but most importantly, to be close to her children and grandchildren.

Grandma is very social and loves speaking to people so Covid-19 was hard for her. She loves cooking and making food for the family and could not do that during the pandemic. However, she is grateful for life and her heart goes out to all those families who have lost loved ones.

By Makai Williams, aged 8

Makai is loving, caring and full of energy. He is very confident and loves performing, being centre stage and is in touch with who he is and how he feels. Makai loves playing chess, watching 'Naruto' and playing computer games like Minecraft. Makai wants to be an author like his older sister, Makaylah Williams, and his father. Makai wants to inspire other people and he wants to make lots of money so he can find homes for the homeless.

Nana
Angela Peart

My nan's name is Angela Maria Peart. She is also known as Jelly because her Dad used to call her An-Jella. She was born on 22 June 1957 in Greenwich Hospital, London.

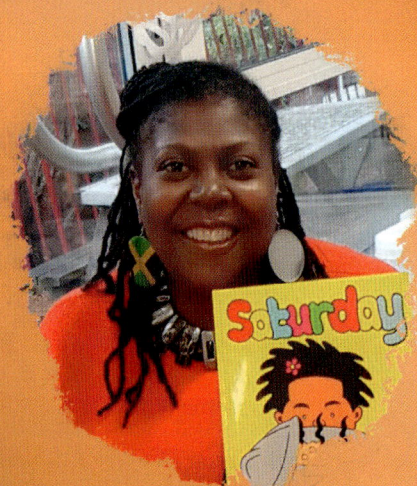

Her mother's name is Lileth Shirley Philips and she was born in Kingston, Jamaica. She moved to England aged 16 and worked in a department store. She then started her own business baking amazing cakes. Her speciality was fruitcake, from a Jamaican tradition, which she passed down to my mum. Nana's father's name is Leroy Phillips and he, too, was born in Kingston, Jamaica. Her father is gifted and skilled with his hands. Skilled at carpentry, painting and electrical engineering – he can do it all. He moved to England when he was 18; one of the Windrush Generation. His first job was in a clock-making factory, which was part of Smiths Industries Ltd. His father (my great-great-grandfather) was called Lawford Phillips; he had his own factory in Jamaica making bicycles.

Nana was the first of five children. Her siblings are Marie, Susan, Dee and Derek. Her mother impacted her life the most, teaching her the values of working hard and raising children. Both her parents worked very hard and saved to buy their first house in Sydenham. It had three floors, but they only lived on one floor! Nana shared one bedroom with all four of her siblings so that her parents could rent the other rooms to help other families who had moved from the Caribbean to London and were struggling to find accommodation due to racism. They didn't have computers, tablets and phones, back in the day, so Nana mostly played with her cousins in the park making up games. On Saturdays, her mother would bake and the whole house would smell of cake, and on Sundays, she would cook Sunday dinner: chicken, rice and peas. And oh, could she sing! When Nana was a teenager, she was in a music group with her friends called 'The Ramells'. They had a popular reggae song called 'Jealousy' that made it to the UK reggae charts in the 1970s. When I was little, she used to sing 'Somewhere Over The Rainbow' to me before I went to bed. I love hearing her sing.

Greenwich, England

When Nana was 19, she got married at St. Bartholomew's Church in Sydenham. She has two children and three grandchildren; I'm the youngest. My mum was named Sabrina, after a character from 'Charlie's Angels' and her brother Daniel was named after Daniel from the Bible. My nana's first job was working in Lloyds Bank as an administration officer, processing cheques. But Nana really loved working with children so she started working in nurseries too. One day, she had saved up enough money to start her own business and open a nursery of her own!

My nan is an author like me! She recently wrote a book called 'Saturday Soup'. It was her first published story and a huge achievement for her. For many years, she dreamed of writing a children's book, but lacked the self-confidence to do it. But having been encouraged to attend a course she was inspired by her children and her brother to write her first story and I'm very glad she did. She has written three books based on experiences with her grandchildren, 'Saturday Soup' (me), 'Same Difference' (Ethan, my brother) and 'Graduation Day' (Joshua, my cousin). In 2018, Nana received an award for her contribution to community through her work in childcare for over 40 years and her voluntary work with The Black Childcare Network, which campaigned for race equality and greater diversity in toys and books in education.

Nana has found Covid-19 horrendous. She said it's painful not seeing her grandchildren and elderly parents for a prolonged period of time. She had to close her nursery and learn technology like Zoom. The supermarket food restrictions reminded her of the stories her parents told her about rationing during wartime. She did love seeing people come together to appreciate the keyworkers though. My nana is a Christian. She said, "My prayers and faith keep me going and I pray for the day I can hug my grandbabies again. I am so thankful for life and my family, and it's been lovely to spend time on video calls being interviewed."

By Melina Ramirez, aged 10

Melina is very kind and makes friends easily. She loves cooking and has learnt to cook some Caribbean dishes. Her hobbies are art and she likes animals. She reads a lot and her favourite books are the 'Lightning Girl' series by Alesha Dixon.

Great-Grandma Reverend Benita Elenora Foster

My great-grandmother's name was Reverend Benita Elenora Foster. She also sometimes went by the name Netty – a nickname given to her by her grandad. She was born on 28 September 1930 in James Hill, Clarendon in Jamaica. Her mother's name was Florence and she was a seamstress who made pretty dresses. Her father's name was Obidiah and he was a farmer that owned seven acres of land and provided all the wood for the first New Testament Church built in James Hill.

Growing up in Jamaica with eight brothers and three sisters, and a boy dog called Blacky, meant the house was full of life. Nana always had a kind heart, even though it sometimes got her into trouble. When she was younger, she would give away yam heads, which they had in the house, to people who she thought needed them – but when it was time to cook them for dinner, there weren't any left to cook!

She was a hard worker too and valued her education. Nana went to school, then college and then Bible school after that, where she graduated as a minister of the gospel. She was a practicing Pentecostal Christian and her faith was very important to her. She said "It's my whole life. My everything." Her favourite book was the Bible, her favourite scripture was Psalm 23, because her mother taught her that she should never want for anything, her favourite hymn was Amazing Grace and her favourite song was 'Glory Bound' – a song about being with God.

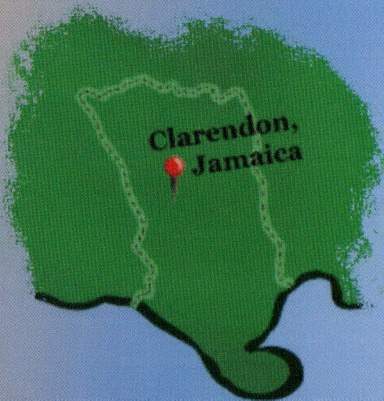

My great-grandmother was the first of her siblings to leave home in James Hill, Jamaica, in search of a new and better life in England. She arrived in the UK in 1952 as one of the Windrush Generation and lived in Forest Hill, South London. She got a job as a nurse and stayed in nursing for 30 years. She lived with her older sister and her sister's husband as it was very hard to find accommodation back then. Her sister's husband introduced her to his friend, my great-grandad; and just three months after meeting each other, they got married in Paddington.

There were only around 50 guests in attendance as they couldn't afford to have a huge wedding and it was difficult to hire a hall. They didn't have a honeymoon either because money was tight.

In total, my great-grandmother had nine children – three boys and six girls, two of whom were adopted. Nana wanted to adopt mostly because of her kind-hearted nature but she also said that with a surname like Foster, how could she not?

Nana liked naming her children after famous people. One of my great-uncles is called Wayne, after the American actor, John Wayne, and my daddy's mum, grandma Beverley, was named after the British pop group, 'The Beverley Sisters'. In total, my great-grandmother had 24 grandchildren and 22 great-grandchildren. She loved being a grandparent very much and said the best thing about it was having all the children around her.

Nana remained dedicated to her faith after she came to England. She was ordained a Reverend and was a member of the New Testament Church of God in Willesden. She was the choir mistress too! She had such a beautiful voice. My family is very big and lots of my relatives inherited my great-grandma's musical talents. One of her sons, Desmond Foster, was in a group called 'Arema' and wrote the No.1 hit record 'In love with you, Darling' and my great-grandmother's niece and daughter were part of the 1970s disco group 'Boney M'.

My wonderful great-grandmother Reverend Benita Elenora Foster, sadly died shortly after I did this interview. I asked my great-grandmother her thoughts and feelings about Covid-19. She believed that the coming of the Lord is near as the Bible said there will be signs and wonders when God is moving – and she believed that Covid-19 is one of those signs.

By Mylee Campbell, aged 9

Mylee has a very bubbly, energetic and outgoing personality. She has a very caring nature and is liked by all her peers, family members (they call her Mylovelee) and teachers, who refer to her as Smiley Mylee! She is a playground ambassador at school and received a Pupil Achievement Award for outstanding progress in mathematics in 2018. Mylee loves watching movies at home and the cinema – her favourite is 'Matilda'. Mylee likes to sing and dance and she attends Pauline Quirke Academy of Performing Arts every Saturday, without fail. She also wanted to add that she loves doing cartwheels!

Grandad Reverend Sean Samuel

My grandad's name is Sean Rupert Athelstan Samuel, also known as Shinkles because he was light-weight when younger. He was born on the 28 August 1961 in Leicester, England. His mum, Veronica Sigretto Samuel, was an accountant at the Half Moon Bay hotel in Antigua. His dad, Rupert Samuel, lectured in mechanics – a trade he learned while he in the RAF. His dad was very strict and he was always getting lectures from him – everything had a place and should be in it. The most important lesson his parents taught him was "Respect other people because if you have manners, you can go a long way in life."

When Grandad was six months old, he moved to Antigua. He was the sixth child of 11 children for his Dad and the sixth of six children for his mum. The family member he remembers most is his Auntie Rita who used to look after him when his mum wasn't around. She was very kind and used to give Grandad pocket money. He used to do chores for her. She taught him that nothing in life is free. She was always happy to see him and still lives in the same house in Antigua with her husband Uncle Ronny.

In Antigua, they don't have cold winters, but they do have rainy season and hurricanes. In his old neighbourhood there were poor and rich areas. His family were lower middle class, so they always had a nice house, running water and electricity. A lot of his friends were very poor, they had to travel to the water pipes to get water for cooking and washing. The thing he remembers most about his childhood was walking around barefoot in the sun and fishing with his uncle. He also remembers how he nearly drowned when he was little and his brother Rory, aka Heads, saved him.

St. John's, Antigua

Grandad went to a Catholic school, St Michael's, and his teachers were nuns. One, Sister Gabriel, was tall, had a croaky voice, was in her sixties and had a lot of loose skin around her neck. She was scary. Another teacher, Mrs Joseph, was a black lady and she had a yard ruler and if you misbehaved, you would get hit on the palm of your hand and if your mum or dad found out that you had been hit at school, you would get beaten at home too for embarrassing them.

His mother was a single parent so he did lots of chores growing up to help out: washing clothes by hand, ironing, cooking and if the lawnmower broke down, he would use a stick or machete to cut the grass in the garden and in Antigua, the gardens are massive. If he skipped his chores, his mum would wake him up in the night to do them. He loved playing too. He used to race pet donkeys with his brothers and he collected marbles – at one point he had hundreds!

When Grandad was 17, he moved to Derby in England. The person who had a great impact on his life was his friend Bishop M.L. Powell. Grandad didn't know his father growing up and Bishop became a father figure to him. He ordained him and gave him his first clergy shirt. Grandad was the last minister he inducted before he died.

Grandad has five children; Leon, Esther, Naomi (my mum whose name means pleasantness), Rachel and Selina. He loves being a grandparent and always talks about the joy we bring him watching us grow and seeing our personalities. Grandad has many favourite foods: stew chicken, his special omelette, Guinness punch, and the famous Samuel mac and cheese. His favourite athlete is Usain Bolt because he's a black man who struggled to get where he has, but succeeded because of commitment.

Grandad feels that Covid-19 is a difficult time with a lot of uncertainty. It has also been an opportunity for people to go back to the old days and be kind, caring and supportive of one another. Due to this pandemic he believes a lot of people may struggle with mental health and anxiety, but it will make people realise how precious human life is.

By Nevaeh Bramwell–Thompson, aged 12

Nevaeh is a valuable member of her family and church community.
She is a high achiever, self-motivated and independent and takes part in extra-curricular activities, and is regularly rewarded for her positive attitude. Trained as a peer mediator, Nevaeh takes the time to help peers with disabilities and additional needs. Nevaeh loves dance, British Sign Language, swimming, piano and basketball. She also takes a leading role in children's service at church – she reads the Bible, encourages other children and is part of a dance group.

Great-Grandma Hilda Joyce Baxter

My great-grandmother's name is Hilda Joyce Baxter (née Passley). She is known as Joyce to all her friends and family – she prefers it to Hilda. Her nickname growing up was Sybil, which is also her mum's name. It became confusing when people called one of them and they both would answer, so that's why she changed her name to Joyce. But I just call her Grandma.

She was born on 9 January 1937 in Port Antonio, Jamaica, to Doris Louise Passley, a dressmaker and Lorenzo Passley, a bespoke tailor. Her father was also an expert cake decorator, farmer, musician, dressmaker and bush doctor. My great-great-grandad could do so many things.

My great-grandma is the older sister by four and a half years. She has one sister called Hazel – they are best, best friends. Once, when they were younger, my great-grandma was left to look after my great-auntie Hazel and they went out to pick mangoes. They were so ripe and juicy and the juice dripped from their face to their clothes. When they ran out of places to dry their sticky hands the only place they could think to use was their hair. They got home all sticky and too full for dinner.

Grandma was a little bit naughty. She would sometimes skip school so she could pick mangoes. She would go to school for half a day and then when it was lunchtime she would leave and then pick mangoes instead of going back to school. Sometimes, she'd bring them home to eat, her mum was pleased with the mangoes but upset that she didn't stay at school. She also got in trouble plenty of times for not doing chores and for mumbling under her breath too!

They didn't have a television at home, only a radio. Grandma would go to the bakery to watch television but not that often because as a little girl she wasn't allowed to stay out very late. She was 16 when she went to her first dance. It was at the wharf, where they shipped bananas and all types of fruit to other countries. She asked her mum if she could go and three other people said they would look after her.

Port Antonio
Jamaica

The three people each gave her mum one shilling to pay for the ticket – but the ticket only cost one shilling so her mum kept two shillings. At the dance they played Rock and Roll music and my great-grandma danced with a few boys. She still likes dancing! At midnight, her mum was waiting by the gate with a sheet to cover her and walk her home.

In 1954, my great-grandma had her first child and called him Raymond Fitzgeorge, she had my grandma Rhowena, next and then Owen in Jamaica. Three more (Elaine, Patrick and Sharon) were born later in England. Her daughter Rachel died at birth but she is always remembered. While she was in Jamaica, my great-grandad decided that they should move to England. It was 1961 and there wasn't enough space for her children to come too so she had to leave her three children behind. She said this was the hardest thing she has ever had to do.

When she arrived in England, she moved to Chapeltown, Leeds and got a job as a dressmaker and a carer. She enjoyed caring the most because she is a very caring person. My great-grandma is very active – she used to roller skate, ride bikes and she was even skateboarding at 53 years old! She even climbed a ladder, aged 82, to sand and paint her front door. She has travelled to many places in the world like Milan, Marrakesh, South America, Panama and the West Indies. She is so cool! Her favourite things are her grandchildren and great-grandchildren, her sister and gardening.

She is very worried about Covid-19 and she really hopes that she doesn't get it because as a black person it seems to be very dangerous. She doesn't understand how we, as black people, are dying so easily in England: "Jamaica has managed to stop the spread of it, like that, but here we are dying in England."

By Niara Pilgrim-Hamilton, aged 9

Niara is shy but determined. She enjoys drawing, more than anything. When she grows up, Niara has her heart set on becoming an astronaut and a famous singer. She is also a keen runner. She enjoys reading the 'Tom Gates' series by Liz Pichon and spending time with her cousins. Niara is one of the funniest people you will meet, she is quick witted and friendly. She has a strong family ethic and loves animals. She lives with her mother and her eldest brother, Kai, is away at university. She has two more brothers, Aiden and Yanel and Freya, her beautiful little sister.

Great-Grandma Ethline Maud Hunter

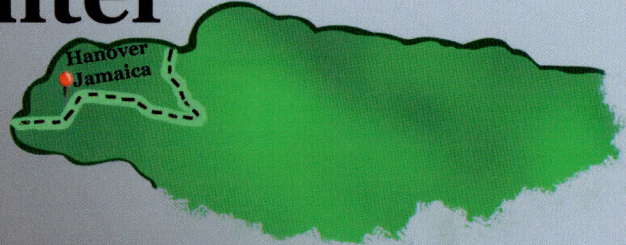

My great-grandma's full name is Ethline Maud Hunter and she was born on 27 July 1929 which means she will be 91 years old this year, 2020. Great-grandma Ethline was born in Kendal, Hanover, Jamaica. Her mother was called Daisy Craig, everyone called her Mamma Daisy, and she was a housewife born in 1905. Her Dad was called Amos Adolphos Craig and he was a road worker born in 1895.

Her maternal grandfather was an English man called George Reid and her paternal great-grandfather was Scottish, his name was Daniel Craig (not James Bond).

My great-grandmother was born in the family home in Kendal, and was the fourth child of 11 children. She remembers her dad being a hardworking, loving man. She said that he took good care of them, but sadly he died young. Great-grandma remembers her mum being caring and nurturing, she was such a good person and kind to everyone. She says that she came from a very loving family, all of her siblings got on well together. They didn't have lots of money, but they had each other and that is all that mattered.

> **"All of her 11 siblings got on well together. They didn't have lots of money, but they had each other and that is all that mattered."**

My great-grandma came to England in 1955 and this is where she got her first ever job as a machinist. She married my great-grandad Erick Melbern Hunter and they had nine children; Pauline (my lovely grandma), Hyacinth, Dawn, Eva, Christine, Caroline, Tony, Derrick and Richard.

Great-grandma has lots of very interesting stories: I was surprised when she told me that she had a sister who was also called Ethline Maud.

Her sister was born the year before in 1928 but sadly passed away. Also, my middle name is Daisy, after my great-great-grandma, Mamma Daisy. My favourite story, which Great-grandma told me, was that she used to own a very special cat, her favourite animal, which could understand everything that Great-grandma said. Other than her cat, Great-grandma's favourite things include: listening to music – she likes Bob Marley and loves to dance; eating Jamaican food – Great-grandma says that if ever there's a day she doesn't want to eat we need to call a doctor; and her absolute most favourite thing ever is being around her friends and family. Great-grandma is a very lovely and sociable woman, she enjoys entertaining people in her home and having lots of happy people around her with plenty of food and drink. Five of her children live in America so she enjoys travelling there to visit them.

My great-grandma is finding Covid-19 difficult because she can't be around people and that is what she loves most, but she is coping as best as she can with it. Every Saturday since lockdown started, my great-grandma dresses up in her best clothes and my uncle takes a picture of her or records a video of her sending a message to her family. She always looks beautiful, like a queen.

Great-grandma says that she is proud that she is still managing to cope at her age of nearly 91. Having to self-isolate has meant that she has had no help and just had to get on with things. My great-grandma is amazing.

By Renell Sergeant, aged 10

Renell is an intelligent, fun, loving, creative, and happy girl. Her family are very important to her and she will do anything she can to help them when needed. She loves making and playing with slime, doing her hair and fashion. If she had her way, she would decorate and redesign her house regularly and wear fashionable clothes with her own unique twist of style. Renell also enjoys cooking and baking. One of Renell's greatest achievements is being a co-author of the book 'Hey, Black Girl! 2'

Nanny Jennifer Hudson

My grandmother's name is Jennifer Hudson. She is also known as Nanny Plum after the character in the television cartoon, 'Ben and Holly' who saves them when they get into trouble. Nanny Plum, like my nan, looks after and protects her family. Nanny was born on 9 April 1966 in Clarendon, Jamaica: a place where the sunset glimmers off the top of the hills with golden rays and beautiful colours. Her mother, Estella, was a district nurse, and her dad, Ken, was a farmer.

Nanny was very happy growing up in Jamaica. She played cricket, football and seesaw in the yard with her siblings and climbed trees too. Her chores were to sweep the yard, feed the pigs, goats and chickens and fetch water from the community tank, all before going to school. Her best friend was Millicent. Other children used to pick on Millicent because she was chubby and her fingers were short, but my nanny, the protector, stood up for her and they became close.

My nanny hasn't lost her accent! She said at night she 'did av one stone wa mi use fi sidung pon' (translation: she had a stone that she used to sit down on) before bed. She'd just sit and watch the fireflies – she called them 'winkies' and 'peenie wallies'.

Growing up, Nanny made dolls using a mango seed as a head, plastic bottles for the body and sticks for arms and legs. She would also go to the sea to catch fish and crabs to eat. To catch crabs, you put your hands underneath the rocks in the water and when the crab pinches your finger, you have to be quick and grab it. The crab would bite the top off some of the children's fingers but it taught them to be quicker next time! On Sundays, Nanny would wait for the bike man, Creamy, to ride by and beep his horn, shouting "Fudgey, fudgey, fudgey!" He sold Nanny's favourite grape nut ice cream and she would save her lunch money to buy some.

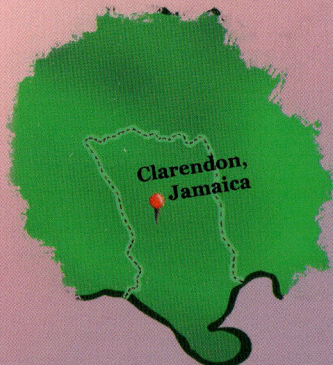

Clarendon, Jamaica

Nanny loved performing and won Louise Bennett's Dialect Poetry competition. Louise Bennett (aka Miss Lou) was famous for her folklore poems that she wrote and recited in Jamaican patois. Nanny wore traditional African attire and performed a poem called 'Dry-foot Bwoy'. For this, she won her first of many awards. My nanny has met a few famous people too like Prince Charles, Will Smith, Jada Pinkett, Alan Sugar and Usain Bolt. Usain is her favourite because he is talented, generous to his community and has put Jamaica on the world map. She was also a good sprinter when she was younger – she was one of the fastest girls in the district of St. Catherine, but injured her knee so couldn't continue competing.

My nanny met my grandad through a mutual friend. They had dinner together and he was very funny and made her smile. She told me that my grandad had a dog named Comin and one day he wanted the dog to go out of the house so he kept shouting "Comin, come out!" The dog was clearly confused. He didn't know whether to come inside or go outside. I could not stop laughing at that story. Nanny and grandad fell in love, got married and had three children who were all born in Jamaica. She named them Cagney and Lacey, after the American television detectives, and Dadrian – my uncle. His name means daydreaming because when was born, he looked exactly like the child she saw in her dreams.

My nanny's favourite bible verse is Psalm 91:1, 'He that dwelleth in the secret place of the most high....' When she reads it, it gives her a sense of security, knowing that she can call upon God in her time of need. She says, "He is my protector and healer."

Nanny is very sad about Covid-19, and her prayers are with the many families who have lost loved ones. She has been very blessed in this pandemic and she gives God the glory for keeping her and her family safe.

By Shaddai Francis, aged 9

Shaddai dances for the Royal Ballet Academy and is in grade 4. She enjoys swimming and attends extracurricular classes in maths and English in her spare time, which she thoroughly enjoys. Shaddai loves reading and writing and won a Young Writers' talent award in 2019 for writing a poem, which was published in a Young Writers' Anthology. She has also written her own book called 'That's Why John Crow's Head's Red'. During the summer holidays she loves going to Jamaica being on the beach, listening to the elders' folklore stories and playing outdoors with other children.

Grandma Maureen Reid

My grandmother's name is Maureen Reid. As a small child, she was given the name Muscle Chicken by family members because she'd flinch like a little chicken when having a shower. She was born at home on 21 May 1952 in Greenwich Town, Kingston, Jamaica and lived in a house with her mother, June, (aka Kitty) and extended family.

Gran's first memory was a sad one. It was Christmas Eve and her grandmother was boiling water for turtle soup, which was a family favourite. Her sister, Rosie, was doing her chores in the kitchen when the stick of the broom hit the oil stove and it fell on her. Rosie and Gran were badly burnt and sadly, Rosie died on Boxing Day.

What my grandmother remembered most about her childhood was mango picking and crab season. As children, they used to sit and wait for the crabs to be cooked, then put salt on the side, crack the shell and eat the meat that was inside. She loved it!

Grandma loved playing! She used to make her own slingshot toys out of wood and elastic to catch birds and knock mangos from trees. She also played vet with all the animals in the yard and would put bandages and splints on the dogs' and chickens' legs. Other games she loved to play were marbles, hopscotch and a game called see, well, lash where you take out the insides of a grapefruit, and fill it with dirt and sing a song as you balanced the fruit on your foot. There was also tick-tack-toe, which was basically 3-D noughts and crosses using pebbles and jacks. If she didn't have proper metal jacks, she'd use pebbles and catch them on the back of her hand. It was a very skilful game.

The toilet in my gran's house was outside. It was like a shed and inside was a big, deep hole in the ground with a toilet seat on top. As a child, she had to tear up newspaper so everyone could use it to wipe their bums. It was full of cockroaches and at night, she would set the paper alight to make the cockroaches run away so she could use the toilet.

Kingston
Jamaica

My grandmother was the middle child of three sisters and her mum went to live in England in 1954. Gran's grandmother looked after her and then her Godfather Gee-Gee, who was loving and very kind, looked after her. Gran joined her mum in England when she was 11 and a half years old. It was strange meeting her mother because she didn't know her that well and hadn't seen her in eight years. Communication had only been through letters. On her first night in England, Gran pretended she forgot her nightclothes hoping her mum would let her go back to Jamaica to get them. She couldn't understand why there wasn't any fruit on the trees: no plums, no guineps and no mangoes.

In her 20s, there was a Black Power Movement when many black people in Britain wanted to be recognised for their achievements and contributions. Gran said she had an afro and wore African gowns. She set up Saturday schools in Peckham and Brixton making sure black children could learn about their history as well as maths and English. My gran wanted to be a doctor but couldn't afford to stay home and study so instead she worked in a bank and then became a social worker, a manager in social services and retired as an independent reviewing officer. It was her passion to support children because she didn't feel she had been supported enough as a child.

My grandma once met Coretta Scott King, Reverend Dr Martin Luther King Jr's wife and her favourite sports person is Usain Bolt because he is Jamaican, fast and humble. Her favourite hobby is gardening because she loves seeing plants grow and her favourite saying is 'tomorrow is another day' because she believes there is no need to stress.

Grandma feels that Covid-19 is very sad because many people have died. She finds the whole situation scary because we have to treat family like we all have a disease.

By Theodore Ashley, aged 12

Theo is a kind, calm young boy, who enjoys playing on his computer, skate boarding and watching/reading anime. His favourite subjects are design technology, art and PE. Theo has never liked writing very much and he was diagnosed with dyslexia in Year 6. However, he has recently shown an interest in writing a book. He has a wonderful imagination and had a poem published in primary school.

Grandma Dolores Edwards

Bradford, England

Our grandma's name is Dolores Edwards. She was born in Bradford, West Yorkshire on 15 February 1963 at Bradford Royal Infirmary. The names of our grandma's parents were Iris Terrelonge and Stephen Terrelonge. Iris was an auxiliary nurse at Bradford Royal Infirmary and Stephen worked at a metal company that was called Hepworth and Grundig. Grandma lived with her family in a block of flats. She was a happy child and loved playing – especially cricket. Just as she was starting Belle Vue Grammar School, Grandma found out she had to move to Jamaica and she wasn't happy at all! She had been really looking forward to going to that school.

When Grandma got to Jamaica she lived in Jones Town with her grandparents. They had a shop and were well known in the community. Grandma also had other family who had shops in the area. When her parents finally bought their own house, they all moved to Harbour View.

> **"Our grandma is a Christian and her favourite verse from the Bible is Ephesians 4:2"**

It was very close to the beach and Grandma had some memorable times there. It was so different to living in Jones Town – her parents taught her to enjoy life. Grandma's favourite toys as a child were her dolls; she played nurses and teachers. When she was younger, she wanted to be a nurse. She started her nursing training in Jamaica but then decided it wasn't for her. Grandma is now a teacher.

Our grandma is a Christian and her favourite verse from the Bible is Ephesians 4:2, 'Be completely humble and gentle; be patient, bearing with one another in love'.

A few years ago, Grandma was diagnosed with breast cancer and she believes that God helped her get over the challenges she faced. She loves being with her family too – it makes her very happy.

The things we found most interesting about Grandma are her three children; two daughters and a son. Grandma says her eldest daughter (our mum) is a warrior mother. She named her Sheneka because of its meanings: 'queen of the pure ones' and 'supreme woman'. Both meanings are derived from two African languages. My uncle opens his heart to give by doing all that he can to help his family and friends whenever they are in need. Plus, he used to pull pranks on my grandma a lot! My youngest aunty has written a poem about Grandma surviving breast cancer – we are very proud of her.

Grandma's favourite artists are Whitney Houston and Beyonce, her favourite colour is iris because her mum's name was Iris. Her favourite animal is a monkey because they can be so mischievous and do things that humans can do.

Because of Covid-19, Grandma says 2020 is a year she will never forget. My Uncle Joseph gave grandma a Mother's Day present and she couldn't give him a hug because of this horrible pandemic. It made her cry. Not being able to be in the same space as her loved ones and spend time with them, or give her children and grandchildren lots of hugs breaks her heart.

By Kiarni and Tiarni Dawkins aged 7 and 8

Tiarni And Kiarni are both happy, cheerful children. They love gymnastics and dancing. They help out in the kitchen and enjoy doing housework and listening to the latest music. They are both very bubbly and intelligent girls and love making videos of themselves.

Grandma Vaida Vongai Makamure

Gutu, Zimbabwe

My grandmother's name was Mrs Vaida Vongai Makamure. She was born at home on 15 May 1935 in Gutu, Zimbabwe. Her mother, Erina, was a housewife and her father, Hakurimwi, was a baker. She was born in a rural village and was the second eldest of six children, who would all describe her as dominant because she used to be a bit bossy and tell them what to do. Her best friend was Dzidzai Chaputsira, who grew up with her.

Her father died when she was very young and her mother was a disciplinarian. Grandma and her siblings learnt very quickly how to entertain themselves. They would make their own toys through various methods. They made dolls by wrapping a cob from an eaten corn on the cob, which were then dressed in used clothes and paraded around. This was Grandma's favourite childhood activity. Much like children today, she did chores too: washing dishes, cleaning the house and fetching water. She also worked in the fields. However, doing chores was an expectation so she never received pocket money for it.

"My Grandma was declared a liberation war heroine by the Zimbabwean government."

Grandma went to live with her aunt and it was there she met her future husband. His name was Danidziral. Her aunt was married to grandpa's uncle. They married in Alheit Mission, Gutu in Zimbabwe and had six children; my mum Vongai was the youngest. Gran's first four children were named after famous people and places (Florence, Wellington, Constance and Winston). She and Grandad believed by giving them these names they would become famous. Her last two children were named after Grandma and Grandad.

Grandma was a really good dancer, she worked as a domestic science teacher and her favourite food was a traditional Zimbabwean dish, rice with peanut butter – you could eat that with anything! My grandfather bought her first car – a Datsun 120Y.

My grandma had the opportunity to travel to other countries, particularly, to Ghana and Germany. She went on a work trip to Germany during Oktoberfest but because she didn't drink alcohol, her work colleagues begged her to take her share and then give her beer to them. She found that really funny. When she visited Ghana, she had to adjust to the food so did not eat much. This meant she ended up losing a lot of weight. Throughout her life she lived in Gutu, Buhera, Morgenster, Gweru, and Masvingo, all beautiful places in Zimbabwe.

Grandma was a devout Christian and believed in praying for everything. Christianity was at the centre of her life. She loved the Lord. Her favourite book was the Bible and she loved the Psalms written by King David. Psalms 23 was her favourite bible chapter and her favourite phrase was "Let's pray about it." She was also politically active, especially during Zimbabwe's liberation struggle. She believed in equality and freedom for everyone and was not afraid to stand up for it. In 2016, after she died, she was declared a liberation war heroine by the Zimbabwean government.

For this profile, I interviewed my mum, who fortunately knew a lot about my grandma and shared a lot of her stories with me. I feel I now know her very well – I was 9 years old when she died, but she visited us a lot in South Africa, which gave me an opportunity to spend a lot of time with her.

By Tinashe Nduna, aged 13

Tinashe is an avid reader. His hobbies include watching old films, anime and reading mystery novels. He likes writing, family gatherings and conversing with friends. His favourite books are the 'Harry Potter' novel series by J. K. Rowling and his favourite film is 'Just Mercy'. His achievements include Headmaster's commendations for history, ICT and mathematics. He recently received a second-grade certificate in poetry for allied arts.

Nana Beverly Steele

My nana's name is Beverley Michele Steele, aka Debbie. She was born on 28 November 1960 in Spanish Town, Jamaica. Her parents are Louise Mitchel and Lester Steele. When Nana was just two years old, her mother left for England to pursue nursing and build a better life for her children. She didn't see her mother again until she came to England aged 11, although she received letters and cards from her.

Nana was raised by her kind grandparents, Nina and James, in a big house on a large piece of land in Spicy Hill, Trelawny. They had mango, banana, coconut and breadfruit trees, as well as yam and a variety of herbs. They owned lots of animals too; cats, pigs, chickens, goats and dogs. Nana had her own dog, called Rex. Before school, she would feed the animals and take the goats to pasture in a field. Nana didn't have toys to keep her occupied, instead she loved collecting shells at the beach, reading, doing crosswords and puzzles. Nana didn't get driven to school like I do, she travelled an hour on foot each way! She enjoyed school though and liked her teachers; especially her head teacher. Nana remembers having a very happy childhood, and that although they all had their little chores to do, she thinks they were quite spoilt.

In 1972, Nana came to England; her memories are of it being cold and grey looking; not colourful like her homeland, Jamaica. She wasn't happy at all. She met her life-long friend Janet in church and they are still best friends today. She went to Islington Green School followed by Islington College and Hackney College. Although school life in England was challenging, she was a great athlete and won awards for the relay, shot put and long jump. Ever the hard worker, Nana was the nominated student representative at college and was even chosen to present awards to deserving students in a special needs school. Later in life, she worked as a lead teaching assistant, supporting students with special educational needs.

Spanish Town
Jamaica

My nana remembers her first date well. Her boyfriend, at the time, took her to an arcade for the first time and she won some money. She can remember rows and rows of colourful machines, the sounds of beeping and chiming pings, the smell of candyfloss and burgers. She had so much fun playing the pinball machine, video games, mechanical claw crane and slot machines that she forgot the time and was late getting back home. I won't say any more about that!

My nana has five children, two boys and three girls. She named her daughters, my aunties, after female African warriors and her last son's name means 'God brought me joy'. She split with her partner when the children were little and raised them by herself.

My nana is the bravest! She's been caving in Wales and has abseiled down the side of a mountain. But the bravest thing she has ever done is beat breast cancer. She was diagnosed before I was born, when she was 36. It was a very scary time for her, but with the support of her doctor, nurses, family, friends and her faith, she pulled through and is still cancer-free 24 years later. Nana said cancer is only a chapter in her life; not the whole story. Her courage gives me strength!

Nana has a long list of favourites. Most important is her faith. She is a Muslim and her favourite Quran verse is the first 'Surah' – a prayer for guidance, lordship and mercy of Allah. If Nana was stuck on a desert island and could only take three things with her, it would probably be her Quran, some reggae music and her crosswords, so she won't get bored!

Nana says that the Covid-19 experience has been an anxious time for her. The news reports were very frightening and government guidelines were not clear. She also felt bored and lonely during lockdown as she was isolating alone and wasn't able to see her family or friends. However, with her fourteen grandchildren, she'd probably feel a bit overwhelmed if they all came round on the same day! But, she loves her family, each and every one of them – to infinity and beyond!

By Ziah Anderson-Steele, aged 12

Ziah is a sweet, sensitive girl with a strong sense of fairness and justice. She's very fond of the outdoors and loves opportunities to connect with nature and animals. She enjoys reading, dancing, gymnastics, creative writing, drawing and adores looking after her cat. She is an avid reader and likes a variety of genres; her preference is humour. One of her favourite books is 'There's a Boy in the Girls Bathroom' by Louis Sachar. Her accomplishments this year include, achieving 100 merits in just 5 days of her first term of secondary school, being shortlisted, and performed with her African dance & drumming group at the Hackney Empire and she also co-wrote her first book, Hey, Black Girl! 2 which was influenced by people who inspire her.

Blackjac Media Publications

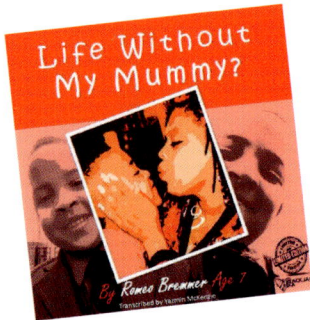

Life Without My Mummy?
By Romeo Bremmer
978-0-9933168-1-4

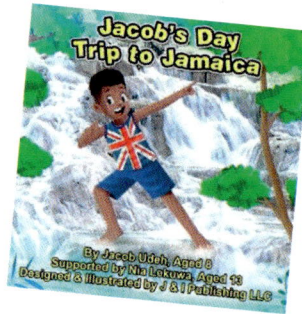

Jacob's Day Trip to Jamaica
By Jacob Udeh & Nia Lekuwa
978-1-9161164-8-1

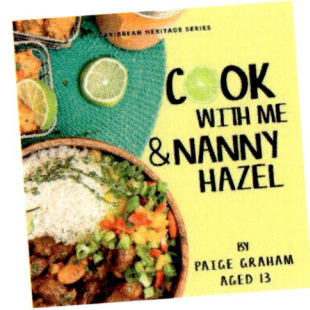

Cook With Me
By Paige Graham
978-1-9161164-1-2

Romeo's Guide to London Architecture
By Romeo Bremmer
978-1-9161164-3-6

Romeo's Guide to Free London for Children 1
By Romeo Bremmer
978-1-9993274-5-3

Romeo's Guide to Free London for Children 2
By Romeo Bremmer
978-1-9993274-7-7

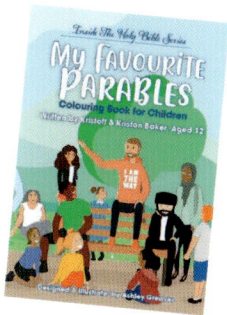

My Favourite Parables
Christian Colouring Book
By Kristoff & Kriston Baker
978-1-9993274-9-1

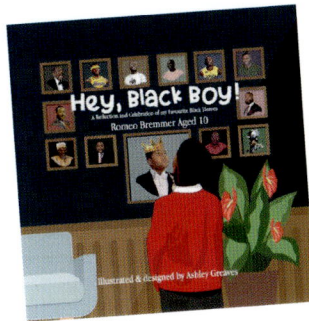

Hey, Black Boy!
By Romeo Bremmer
978-0-9933168-8-3

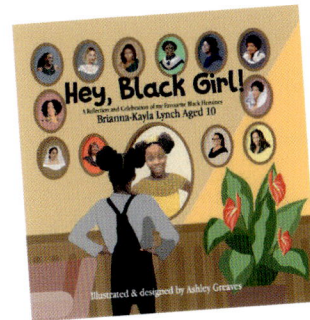

Hey, Black Girl!
By Brianna-Kayla Lynch
978-0-9933168-6-9

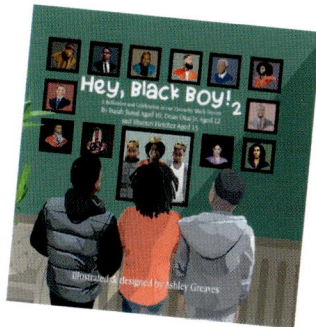

Hey, Black Boy! 2
By Isaiah Jamal, Dean Okai
Jr. and Shamari Fletcher
978-1-9161164-5-0

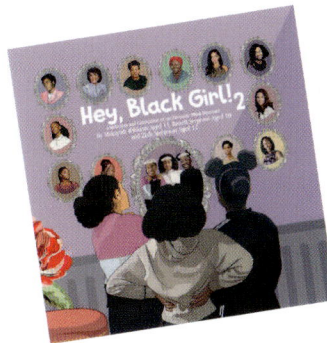

Hey, Black Girl! 2
By Makayla Williams, Renell
Sergeant and Ziah Anderson
978-1-8380945-0-8

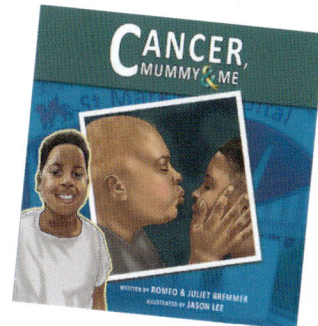

Cancer, Mummy & Me
By Romeo & Juliet Bremmer
978-1-9161164-2-9

**25 Grandparents | 52 to 90 years | 10 Grandfathers
12 Grandmothers | 3 Great Grandmothers**

**From Antigua | Barbados | Derby | Dominica
Greenwich, London | Grenada | Haringey, London | Jamaica
Leicester, UK | Nigeria | Trinidad | Yorkshire | Zimbabwe**